50 Peruvian Cake Recipes

By: Kelly Johnson

Table of Contents

- Torta de Tres Leches (Three Milk Cake)
- Torta de Chocolate Peruana (Peruvian Chocolate Cake)
- Torta Helada (Frozen Cake)
- Torta de Naranja (Orange Cake)
- Torta de Acelga (Chard Cake)
- Torta de Manzana (Apple Cake)
- Torta de Alfajor (Alfajor Cake)
- Torta de Limón (Lemon Cake)
- Torta de Moras (Berry Cake)
- Torta de Pera (Pear Cake)
- Torta de Zanahoria (Carrot Cake)
- Torta de Durazno (Peach Cake)
- Torta de Plátano (Banana Cake)
- Torta de Anís (Anise Cake)
- Torta de Café (Coffee Cake)
- Torta de Miel (Honey Cake)
- Torta de Coco (Coconut Cake)
- Torta de Fresa (Strawberry Cake)
- Torta de Piña (Pineapple Cake)
- Torta de Uva (Grape Cake)
- Torta de Camote (Sweet Potato Cake)
- Torta de Maracuya (Passion Fruit Cake)
- Torta de Vainilla (Vanilla Cake)
- Torta de Chocolate y Nuez (Chocolate and Nut Cake)
- Torta de Chirimoya (Cherimoya Cake)
- Torta de Frambuesa (Raspberry Cake)
- Torta de Papaya (Papaya Cake)
- Torta de Avocado (Avocado Cake)
- Torta de Maca (Maca Root Cake)
- Torta de Quinua (Quinoa Cake)
- Torta de Choclo (Corn Cake)
- Torta de Higo (Fig Cake)
- Torta de Algarrobo (Carob Cake)
- Torta de Galleta (Cookie Cake)

- Torta de Acelga y Queso (Chard and Cheese Cake)
- Torta de Chocoteja (Chocolate-covered Fruit Cake)
- Torta de Lúcuma (Lucuma Cake)
- Torta de Granadilla (Granadilla Cake)
- Torta de Uchuva (Goldenberry Cake)
- Torta de Frutos Rojos (Red Fruits Cake)
- Torta de Lentejas (Lentil Cake)
- Torta de Pargo (Fish Cake)
- Torta de Ají Amarillo (Yellow Chili Cake)
- Torta de Pargo y Camarones (Fish and Shrimp Cake)
- Torta de Tamal (Tamal Cake)
- Torta de Durazno y Maracuyá (Peach and Passion Fruit Cake)
- Torta de Choclo y Queso (Corn and Cheese Cake)
- Torta de Frutos Secos (Dried Fruit Cake)
- Torta de Turrón (Nougat Cake)
- Torta de Café y Canela (Coffee and Cinnamon Cake)

Torta de Tres Leches (Three Milk Cake)

Ingredients:

- **For the cake:**
    - 1 cup all-purpose flour
    - 1 1/2 teaspoons baking powder
    - 1/4 teaspoon salt
    - 5 large eggs, separated
    - 1 cup granulated sugar
    - 1/2 cup whole milk
    - 1/4 cup unsalted butter, melted
    - 1 teaspoon vanilla extract
- **For the milk mixture:**
    - 1 cup evaporated milk
    - 1 cup sweetened condensed milk
    - 1/2 cup whole milk
- **For the topping:**
    - 1 cup heavy cream
    - 1/4 cup powdered sugar
    - 1 teaspoon vanilla extract

Instructions:

1. **Make the cake**: Preheat the oven to 350°F (175°C). Grease and flour a 9x13-inch baking dish.
2. In a bowl, whisk flour, baking powder, and salt. In another bowl, beat egg yolks and sugar until light and fluffy. Add milk, butter, and vanilla, and mix well. Gradually fold in the dry ingredients.
3. In a separate bowl, beat the egg whites until stiff peaks form. Gently fold the egg whites into the batter.
4. Pour the batter into the prepared baking dish and bake for 25-30 minutes, or until a toothpick inserted comes out clean.
5. **Make the milk mixture**: In a bowl, combine evaporated milk, sweetened condensed milk, and whole milk.
6. Once the cake has cooled slightly, poke holes all over the surface with a fork. Slowly pour the milk mixture over the cake and allow it to soak in.

7. **Make the topping**: In a bowl, beat heavy cream, powdered sugar, and vanilla until stiff peaks form. Spread the whipped cream on top of the cake and refrigerate for at least 2 hours before serving.

Torta de Chocolate Peruana (Peruvian Chocolate Cake)

Ingredients:

- 1 1/2 cups all-purpose flour
- 1/2 cup unsweetened cocoa powder
- 1 1/2 teaspoons baking powder
- 1/2 teaspoon baking soda
- 1/4 teaspoon salt
- 1/2 cup unsalted butter, softened
- 1 cup granulated sugar
- 2 large eggs
- 1 teaspoon vanilla extract
- 1 cup whole milk
- 1/2 cup strong brewed coffee
- 1/2 cup dark chocolate chips
- **For the ganache topping:**
    - 1/2 cup heavy cream
    - 4 oz dark chocolate, chopped

Instructions:

1. **Make the cake**: Preheat the oven to 350°F (175°C). Grease and flour an 8-inch round cake pan.
2. In a bowl, whisk together flour, cocoa powder, baking powder, baking soda, and salt.
3. In another bowl, beat butter and sugar until light and fluffy. Add eggs, one at a time, and vanilla. Alternate adding the dry ingredients and milk, mixing until combined. Stir in coffee and chocolate chips.
4. Pour the batter into the prepared pan and bake for 30-35 minutes, or until a toothpick inserted comes out clean. Let cool completely.
5. **Make the ganache**: In a small saucepan, heat heavy cream over medium heat until just simmering. Pour over the chopped chocolate and stir until smooth.
6. Pour the ganache over the cooled cake and let it set before serving.

Torta Helada (Frozen Cake)

Ingredients:

- **For the cake layers:**
    - 1 box of sponge cake or ladyfingers (about 24 pieces)
    - 1/2 cup strong brewed coffee or milk
- **For the filling:**
    - 2 cups heavy cream
    - 1 cup sweetened condensed milk
    - 1 teaspoon vanilla extract
    - 1/2 cup cocoa powder
    - 1/2 cup dark chocolate, chopped

Instructions:

1. **Prepare the cake layers**: Dip the sponge cake or ladyfingers into the coffee or milk and line the bottom and sides of a springform pan.
2. **Make the filling**: In a bowl, whip the heavy cream until stiff peaks form. In another bowl, whisk together the sweetened condensed milk, vanilla, and cocoa powder. Gently fold in the whipped cream.
3. Stir in chopped chocolate and spread the filling over the prepared cake layers. Top with another layer of dipped cake.
4. Freeze for at least 4 hours or until firm. Before serving, let the cake sit at room temperature for 10-15 minutes to soften slightly.

Torta de Naranja (Orange Cake)

Ingredients:

- 1 1/2 cups all-purpose flour
- 1 1/2 teaspoons baking powder
- 1/2 teaspoon salt
- 1/2 cup unsalted butter, softened
- 1 cup granulated sugar
- 2 large eggs
- 1 teaspoon vanilla extract
- 1/2 cup fresh orange juice
- 1 tablespoon orange zest
- **For the glaze:**
    - 1/2 cup powdered sugar
    - 2 tablespoons fresh orange juice

Instructions:

1. **Make the cake**: Preheat the oven to 350°F (175°C). Grease and flour an 8-inch round cake pan.
2. In a bowl, whisk together flour, baking powder, and salt.
3. In a separate bowl, beat butter and sugar until light and fluffy. Add eggs one at a time, mixing well after each. Stir in vanilla, orange juice, and orange zest.
4. Gradually add the dry ingredients and mix until just combined.
5. Pour the batter into the prepared pan and bake for 30-35 minutes, or until a toothpick inserted comes out clean.
6. **Make the glaze**: In a small bowl, whisk together powdered sugar and orange juice. Drizzle the glaze over the cooled cake before serving.

Torta de Acelga (Chard Cake)

Ingredients:

- 2 cups fresh chard, chopped
- 1 1/2 cups all-purpose flour
- 1 teaspoon baking powder
- 1/2 teaspoon salt
- 1 cup granulated sugar
- 1/2 cup unsalted butter, softened
- 3 large eggs
- 1 teaspoon vanilla extract
- 1/2 cup milk
- Powdered sugar for dusting (optional)

Instructions:

1. Preheat the oven to 350°F (175°C). Grease and flour an 8-inch cake pan.
2. In a bowl, mix flour, baking powder, and salt.
3. In another bowl, beat butter and sugar until light and fluffy. Add eggs, one at a time, and vanilla.
4. Gradually add the dry ingredients and milk, mixing until smooth. Stir in the chopped chard.
5. Pour the batter into the prepared pan and bake for 30-35 minutes, or until a toothpick inserted comes out clean.
6. Let the cake cool before dusting with powdered sugar and serving.

Torta de Manzana (Apple Cake)

Ingredients:

- 2 cups all-purpose flour
- 1 teaspoon baking powder
- 1/2 teaspoon baking soda
- 1/2 teaspoon cinnamon
- 1/4 teaspoon salt
- 1 cup granulated sugar
- 1/2 cup unsalted butter, softened
- 2 large eggs
- 1 teaspoon vanilla extract
- 2 medium apples, peeled and chopped
- 1/2 cup chopped walnuts (optional)

Instructions:

1. Preheat the oven to 350°F (175°C). Grease and flour an 8-inch round cake pan.
2. In a bowl, whisk together flour, baking powder, baking soda, cinnamon, and salt.
3. In a separate bowl, beat butter and sugar until light and fluffy. Add eggs, one at a time, and vanilla.
4. Gradually add the dry ingredients and mix until combined. Fold in the chopped apples and walnuts.
5. Pour the batter into the prepared pan and bake for 30-35 minutes, or until a toothpick inserted comes out clean.
6. Let the cake cool before serving.

Torta de Alfajor (Alfajor Cake)

Ingredients:

- 1 box of Alfajor cookies (or homemade, filled with dulce de leche)
- 1 1/2 cups heavy cream
- 1 tablespoon powdered sugar
- 1 teaspoon vanilla extract
- 1 cup dulce de leche
- Powdered sugar for dusting

Instructions:

1. **Assemble the cake**: Arrange a layer of Alfajor cookies at the bottom of a springform pan. Spread a thin layer of dulce de leche on top. Repeat the process with the remaining cookies and dulce de leche.
2. In a bowl, beat the heavy cream with powdered sugar and vanilla until stiff peaks form. Spread the whipped cream on top of the assembled cake.
3. Refrigerate for at least 4 hours, preferably overnight, before serving. Dust with powdered sugar before serving.

Torta de Limón (Lemon Cake)

Ingredients:

- 1 1/2 cups all-purpose flour
- 1 teaspoon baking powder
- 1/2 teaspoon salt
- 1 cup granulated sugar
- 1/2 cup unsalted butter, softened
- 2 large eggs
- 1/2 cup fresh lemon juice
- 1 tablespoon lemon zest
- 1/2 cup milk
- **For the glaze:**
    - 1 cup powdered sugar
    - 2 tablespoons fresh lemon juice

Instructions:

1. Preheat the oven to 350°F (175°C). Grease and flour an 8-inch round cake pan.
2. In a bowl, whisk together flour, baking powder, and salt.
3. In another bowl, beat butter and sugar until light and fluffy. Add eggs, one at a time, and mix well. Stir in lemon juice and zest.
4. Gradually add the dry ingredients and milk, mixing until just combined.
5. Pour the batter into the prepared pan and bake for 30-35 minutes, or until a toothpick inserted comes out clean.
6. **Make the glaze**: In a bowl, whisk together powdered sugar and lemon juice. Drizzle over the cooled cake before serving.

Torta de Moras (Berry Cake)

Ingredients:

- 1 1/2 cups all-purpose flour
- 1 1/2 teaspoons baking powder
- 1/4 teaspoon salt
- 1/2 cup unsalted butter, softened
- 1 cup granulated sugar
- 2 large eggs
- 1 teaspoon vanilla extract
- 1/2 cup milk
- 2 cups mixed berries (blueberries, raspberries, blackberries)
- 1 tablespoon lemon zest
- 1 tablespoon cornstarch (for dusting berries)

Instructions:

1. Preheat the oven to 350°F (175°C). Grease and flour a 9-inch round cake pan.
2. In a bowl, whisk together flour, baking powder, and salt.
3. In another bowl, beat butter and sugar until light and fluffy. Add eggs, one at a time, and vanilla.
4. Gradually add the dry ingredients and milk, mixing until smooth.
5. Gently fold in the berries that have been dusted with cornstarch and lemon zest.
6. Pour the batter into the prepared pan and bake for 30-35 minutes, or until a toothpick inserted comes out clean.
7. Let the cake cool before serving.

Torta de Pera (Pear Cake)

Ingredients:

- 1 1/2 cups all-purpose flour
- 1 teaspoon baking powder
- 1/2 teaspoon cinnamon
- 1/4 teaspoon salt
- 1/2 cup unsalted butter, softened
- 1 cup granulated sugar
- 2 large eggs
- 1 teaspoon vanilla extract
- 2 ripe pears, peeled and sliced
- 1/2 cup milk

Instructions:

1. Preheat the oven to 350°F (175°C). Grease and flour a 9-inch round cake pan.
2. In a bowl, whisk together flour, baking powder, cinnamon, and salt.
3. In another bowl, beat butter and sugar until light and fluffy. Add eggs, one at a time, and vanilla.
4. Gradually add the dry ingredients and milk, mixing until smooth.
5. Fold in the sliced pears and pour the batter into the prepared pan.
6. Bake for 30-35 minutes, or until a toothpick inserted comes out clean.
7. Let the cake cool before serving.

Torta de Zanahoria (Carrot Cake)

Ingredients:

- 2 cups all-purpose flour
- 1 1/2 teaspoons baking powder
- 1 teaspoon baking soda
- 1/2 teaspoon salt
- 1 1/2 teaspoons ground cinnamon
- 1/2 teaspoon ground nutmeg
- 1 1/2 cups granulated sugar
- 1/2 cup unsalted butter, softened
- 4 large eggs
- 2 teaspoons vanilla extract
- 2 cups grated carrots
- 1/2 cup chopped walnuts (optional)
- **For the cream cheese frosting:**
    - 8 oz cream cheese, softened
    - 1/4 cup unsalted butter, softened
    - 2 cups powdered sugar
    - 1 teaspoon vanilla extract

Instructions:

1. Preheat the oven to 350°F (175°C). Grease and flour a 9-inch round cake pan.
2. In a bowl, whisk together flour, baking powder, baking soda, salt, cinnamon, and nutmeg.
3. In another bowl, beat butter and sugar until light and fluffy. Add eggs one at a time, mixing well after each. Stir in vanilla and grated carrots.
4. Gradually add the dry ingredients and mix until combined. Fold in walnuts if using.
5. Pour the batter into the prepared pan and bake for 35-40 minutes, or until a toothpick inserted comes out clean.
6. Let the cake cool completely.
7. **Make the frosting**: In a bowl, beat cream cheese and butter until smooth. Gradually add powdered sugar and vanilla and beat until creamy. Frost the cooled cake and serve.

Torta de Durazno (Peach Cake)

Ingredients:

- 1 1/2 cups all-purpose flour
- 1 1/2 teaspoons baking powder
- 1/4 teaspoon salt
- 1/2 cup unsalted butter, softened
- 1 cup granulated sugar
- 2 large eggs
- 1 teaspoon vanilla extract
- 1/2 cup milk
- 2 ripe peaches, peeled and sliced
- 1 tablespoon lemon juice

Instructions:

1. Preheat the oven to 350°F (175°C). Grease and flour an 8-inch round cake pan.
2. In a bowl, whisk together flour, baking powder, and salt.
3. In another bowl, beat butter and sugar until light and fluffy. Add eggs, one at a time, and vanilla.
4. Gradually add the dry ingredients and milk, mixing until smooth.
5. Gently fold in the peach slices and lemon juice.
6. Pour the batter into the prepared pan and bake for 30-35 minutes, or until a toothpick inserted comes out clean.
7. Let the cake cool before serving.

Torta de Plátano (Banana Cake)

Ingredients:

- 2 cups all-purpose flour
- 1 teaspoon baking powder
- 1/2 teaspoon baking soda
- 1/2 teaspoon salt
- 1/2 teaspoon ground cinnamon
- 1 cup granulated sugar
- 1/2 cup unsalted butter, softened
- 2 large eggs
- 4 ripe bananas, mashed
- 1 teaspoon vanilla extract
- 1/2 cup milk
- **For the cream cheese frosting:**
    - 8 oz cream cheese, softened
    - 1/4 cup unsalted butter, softened
    - 2 cups powdered sugar
    - 1 teaspoon vanilla extract

Instructions:

1. Preheat the oven to 350°F (175°C). Grease and flour a 9-inch round cake pan.
2. In a bowl, whisk together flour, baking powder, baking soda, salt, and cinnamon.
3. In another bowl, beat butter and sugar until light and fluffy. Add eggs one at a time, mixing well after each. Stir in mashed bananas and vanilla.
4. Gradually add the dry ingredients and milk, mixing until smooth.
5. Pour the batter into the prepared pan and bake for 30-35 minutes, or until a toothpick inserted comes out clean.
6. Let the cake cool completely.
7. **Make the frosting**: In a bowl, beat cream cheese and butter until smooth. Gradually add powdered sugar and vanilla and beat until creamy. Frost the cooled cake and serve.

Torta de Anís (Anise Cake)

Ingredients:

- 1 1/2 cups all-purpose flour
- 1 teaspoon baking powder
- 1/2 teaspoon salt
- 1/2 cup unsalted butter, softened
- 1 cup granulated sugar
- 3 large eggs
- 1 teaspoon vanilla extract
- 1 teaspoon anise extract
- 1/2 cup milk

Instructions:

1. Preheat the oven to 350°F (175°C). Grease and flour an 8-inch round cake pan.
2. In a bowl, whisk together flour, baking powder, and salt.
3. In another bowl, beat butter and sugar until light and fluffy. Add eggs, one at a time, mixing well after each. Stir in vanilla and anise extract.
4. Gradually add the dry ingredients and milk, mixing until smooth.
5. Pour the batter into the prepared pan and bake for 25-30 minutes, or until a toothpick inserted comes out clean.
6. Let the cake cool before serving.

Torta de Café (Coffee Cake)

Ingredients:

- 2 cups all-purpose flour
- 1 teaspoon baking powder
- 1/2 teaspoon baking soda
- 1/2 teaspoon salt
- 1/2 cup unsalted butter, softened
- 1 cup granulated sugar
- 2 large eggs
- 1 teaspoon vanilla extract
- 1 cup brewed coffee, cooled
- 1/2 teaspoon ground cinnamon
- 1/4 cup chopped walnuts (optional)

Instructions:

1. Preheat the oven to 350°F (175°C). Grease and flour a 9-inch round cake pan.
2. In a bowl, whisk together flour, baking powder, baking soda, salt, and cinnamon.
3. In another bowl, beat butter and sugar until light and fluffy. Add eggs, one at a time, mixing well after each. Stir in vanilla and brewed coffee.
4. Gradually add the dry ingredients and mix until smooth.
5. Pour the batter into the prepared pan and sprinkle chopped walnuts on top.
6. Bake for 30-35 minutes, or until a toothpick inserted comes out clean.
7. Let the cake cool before serving.

Torta de Miel (Honey Cake)

Ingredients:

- 2 cups all-purpose flour
- 1 teaspoon baking powder
- 1/2 teaspoon baking soda
- 1/2 teaspoon ground cinnamon
- 1/4 teaspoon salt
- 1/2 cup unsalted butter, softened
- 1 cup granulated sugar
- 1/2 cup honey
- 2 large eggs
- 1 teaspoon vanilla extract
- 1/2 cup milk

Instructions:

1. Preheat the oven to 350°F (175°C). Grease and flour an 8-inch round cake pan.
2. In a bowl, whisk together flour, baking powder, baking soda, cinnamon, and salt.
3. In another bowl, beat butter and sugar until light and fluffy. Add honey, eggs, and vanilla, and mix well.
4. Gradually add the dry ingredients and milk, mixing until smooth.
5. Pour the batter into the prepared pan and bake for 30-35 minutes, or until a toothpick inserted comes out clean.
6. Let the cake cool before serving.

Torta de Coco (Coconut Cake)

Ingredients:

- 1 1/2 cups all-purpose flour
- 1 teaspoon baking powder
- 1/4 teaspoon salt
- 1 cup granulated sugar
- 1/2 cup unsalted butter, softened
- 2 large eggs
- 1 teaspoon vanilla extract
- 1/2 cup coconut milk
- 1 cup shredded coconut

Instructions:

1. Preheat the oven to 350°F (175°C). Grease and flour an 8-inch round cake pan.
2. In a bowl, whisk together flour, baking powder, and salt.
3. In another bowl, beat butter and sugar until light and fluffy. Add eggs, one at a time, mixing well after each. Stir in vanilla and coconut milk.
4. Gradually add the dry ingredients and mix until smooth. Fold in shredded coconut.
5. Pour the batter into the prepared pan and bake for 30-35 minutes, or until a toothpick inserted comes out clean.
6. Let the cake cool before serving.

Torta de Fresa (Strawberry Cake)

Ingredients:

- 2 cups all-purpose flour
- 1 1/2 teaspoons baking powder
- 1/4 teaspoon salt
- 1/2 cup unsalted butter, softened
- 1 cup granulated sugar
- 2 large eggs
- 1 teaspoon vanilla extract
- 1/2 cup milk
- 1 1/2 cups fresh strawberries, chopped
- 1 tablespoon lemon zest
- 1/4 cup strawberry jam (optional)

Instructions:

1. Preheat the oven to 350°F (175°C). Grease and flour an 8-inch round cake pan.
2. In a bowl, whisk together flour, baking powder, and salt.
3. In another bowl, beat butter and sugar until light and fluffy. Add eggs, one at a time, and vanilla.
4. Gradually add the dry ingredients and milk, mixing until smooth.
5. Gently fold in the chopped strawberries and lemon zest.
6. Pour the batter into the prepared pan and bake for 30-35 minutes, or until a toothpick inserted comes out clean.
7. Let the cake cool completely, then optionally spread strawberry jam on top before serving.

Torta de Piña (Pineapple Cake)

Ingredients:

- 1 1/2 cups all-purpose flour
- 1 1/2 teaspoons baking powder
- 1/2 teaspoon baking soda
- 1/4 teaspoon salt
- 1/2 cup unsalted butter, softened
- 1 cup granulated sugar
- 2 large eggs
- 1 teaspoon vanilla extract
- 1 cup crushed pineapple, drained
- 1/2 cup coconut flakes (optional)

Instructions:

1. Preheat the oven to 350°F (175°C). Grease and flour an 8-inch round cake pan.
2. In a bowl, whisk together flour, baking powder, baking soda, and salt.
3. In another bowl, beat butter and sugar until light and fluffy. Add eggs, one at a time, and vanilla.
4. Gradually add the dry ingredients and mix until smooth.
5. Fold in the pineapple and coconut flakes if using.
6. Pour the batter into the prepared pan and bake for 30-35 minutes, or until a toothpick inserted comes out clean.
7. Let the cake cool before serving.

Torta de Uva (Grape Cake)

Ingredients:

- 2 cups all-purpose flour
- 1 1/2 teaspoons baking powder
- 1/2 teaspoon salt
- 1/2 cup unsalted butter, softened
- 1 cup granulated sugar
- 2 large eggs
- 1 teaspoon vanilla extract
- 1/2 cup milk
- 1 1/2 cups seedless grapes, halved
- 1 tablespoon lemon zest

Instructions:

1. Preheat the oven to 350°F (175°C). Grease and flour an 8-inch round cake pan.
2. In a bowl, whisk together flour, baking powder, and salt.
3. In another bowl, beat butter and sugar until light and fluffy. Add eggs, one at a time, and vanilla.
4. Gradually add the dry ingredients and milk, mixing until smooth.
5. Gently fold in the halved grapes and lemon zest.
6. Pour the batter into the prepared pan and bake for 30-35 minutes, or until a toothpick inserted comes out clean.
7. Let the cake cool before serving.

Torta de Camote (Sweet Potato Cake)

Ingredients:

- 2 cups all-purpose flour
- 1 teaspoon baking powder
- 1/2 teaspoon baking soda
- 1/2 teaspoon cinnamon
- 1/4 teaspoon nutmeg
- 1/2 teaspoon salt
- 1 cup mashed sweet potatoes (about 2 medium sweet potatoes)
- 1/2 cup unsalted butter, softened
- 1 cup granulated sugar
- 2 large eggs
- 1 teaspoon vanilla extract
- 1/2 cup milk

Instructions:

1. Preheat the oven to 350°F (175°C). Grease and flour an 8-inch round cake pan.
2. In a bowl, whisk together flour, baking powder, baking soda, cinnamon, nutmeg, and salt.
3. In another bowl, beat butter and sugar until light and fluffy. Add eggs, one at a time, and vanilla.
4. Stir in the mashed sweet potatoes and mix until smooth.
5. Gradually add the dry ingredients and milk, mixing until well combined.
6. Pour the batter into the prepared pan and bake for 35-40 minutes, or until a toothpick inserted comes out clean.
7. Let the cake cool before serving.

Torta de Maracuya (Passion Fruit Cake)

Ingredients:

- 1 1/2 cups all-purpose flour
- 1 1/2 teaspoons baking powder
- 1/2 teaspoon salt
- 1/2 cup unsalted butter, softened
- 1 cup granulated sugar
- 2 large eggs
- 1 teaspoon vanilla extract
- 1/2 cup passion fruit juice (fresh or bottled)
- 1 tablespoon lemon zest

Instructions:

1. Preheat the oven to 350°F (175°C). Grease and flour an 8-inch round cake pan.
2. In a bowl, whisk together flour, baking powder, and salt.
3. In another bowl, beat butter and sugar until light and fluffy. Add eggs, one at a time, and vanilla.
4. Gradually add the dry ingredients and passion fruit juice, mixing until smooth.
5. Fold in the lemon zest.
6. Pour the batter into the prepared pan and bake for 30-35 minutes, or until a toothpick inserted comes out clean.
7. Let the cake cool before serving.

Torta de Vainilla (Vanilla Cake)

Ingredients:

- 2 cups all-purpose flour
- 1 1/2 teaspoons baking powder
- 1/2 teaspoon salt
- 1/2 cup unsalted butter, softened
- 1 cup granulated sugar
- 3 large eggs
- 2 teaspoons vanilla extract
- 1/2 cup milk

Instructions:

1. Preheat the oven to 350°F (175°C). Grease and flour an 8-inch round cake pan.
2. In a bowl, whisk together flour, baking powder, and salt.
3. In another bowl, beat butter and sugar until light and fluffy. Add eggs, one at a time, and vanilla.
4. Gradually add the dry ingredients and milk, mixing until smooth.
5. Pour the batter into the prepared pan and bake for 25-30 minutes, or until a toothpick inserted comes out clean.
6. Let the cake cool before serving.

Torta de Chocolate y Nuez (Chocolate and Nut Cake)

Ingredients:

- 1 1/2 cups all-purpose flour
- 1 teaspoon baking powder
- 1/2 teaspoon salt
- 1/2 cup unsalted butter, softened
- 1 cup granulated sugar
- 2 large eggs
- 1 teaspoon vanilla extract
- 1/2 cup cocoa powder
- 1/2 cup chopped nuts (walnuts or pecans)
- 1/2 cup milk

Instructions:

1. Preheat the oven to 350°F (175°C). Grease and flour an 8-inch round cake pan.
2. In a bowl, whisk together flour, baking powder, salt, and cocoa powder.
3. In another bowl, beat butter and sugar until light and fluffy. Add eggs, one at a time, and vanilla.
4. Gradually add the dry ingredients and milk, mixing until smooth.
5. Fold in the chopped nuts.
6. Pour the batter into the prepared pan and bake for 30-35 minutes, or until a toothpick inserted comes out clean.
7. Let the cake cool before serving.

Torta de Chirimoya (Cherimoya Cake)

Ingredients:

- 2 cups all-purpose flour
- 1 1/2 teaspoons baking powder
- 1/2 teaspoon salt
- 1/2 cup unsalted butter, softened
- 1 cup granulated sugar
- 2 large eggs
- 1 teaspoon vanilla extract
- 1 cup cherimoya pulp (from a ripe cherimoya)
- 1/2 cup milk

Instructions:

1. Preheat the oven to 350°F (175°C). Grease and flour an 8-inch round cake pan.
2. In a bowl, whisk together flour, baking powder, and salt.
3. In another bowl, beat butter and sugar until light and fluffy. Add eggs, one at a time, and vanilla.
4. Gradually add the dry ingredients and milk, mixing until smooth.
5. Gently fold in the cherimoya pulp.
6. Pour the batter into the prepared pan and bake for 30-35 minutes, or until a toothpick inserted comes out clean.
7. Let the cake cool before serving.

Torta de Frambuesa (Raspberry Cake)

Ingredients:

- 2 cups all-purpose flour
- 1 1/2 teaspoons baking powder
- 1/2 teaspoon salt
- 1/2 cup unsalted butter, softened
- 1 cup granulated sugar
- 2 large eggs
- 1 teaspoon vanilla extract
- 1/2 cup milk
- 1 1/2 cups fresh raspberries
- 1 tablespoon lemon zest

Instructions:

1. Preheat the oven to 350°F (175°C). Grease and flour an 8-inch round cake pan.
2. In a bowl, whisk together flour, baking powder, and salt.
3. In another bowl, beat butter and sugar until light and fluffy. Add eggs, one at a time, and vanilla.
4. Gradually add the dry ingredients and milk, mixing until smooth.
5. Gently fold in the raspberries and lemon zest.
6. Pour the batter into the prepared pan and bake for 30-35 minutes, or until a toothpick inserted comes out clean.
7. Let the cake cool before serving.

Torta de Papaya (Papaya Cake)

Ingredients:

- 2 cups all-purpose flour
- 1 1/2 teaspoons baking powder
- 1/2 teaspoon salt
- 1/2 cup unsalted butter, softened
- 1 cup granulated sugar
- 2 large eggs
- 1 teaspoon vanilla extract
- 1 cup papaya puree (from ripe papaya)
- 1/4 cup chopped nuts (optional)

Instructions:

1. Preheat the oven to 350°F (175°C). Grease and flour an 8-inch round cake pan.
2. In a bowl, whisk together flour, baking powder, and salt.
3. In another bowl, beat butter and sugar until light and fluffy. Add eggs, one at a time, and vanilla.
4. Gradually add the dry ingredients and papaya puree, mixing until smooth.
5. If desired, fold in the chopped nuts.
6. Pour the batter into the prepared pan and bake for 30-35 minutes, or until a toothpick inserted comes out clean.
7. Let the cake cool before serving.

Torta de Avocado (Avocado Cake)

Ingredients:

- 2 cups all-purpose flour
- 1 1/2 teaspoons baking powder
- 1/2 teaspoon baking soda
- 1/4 teaspoon salt
- 1/2 cup unsalted butter, softened
- 1 cup granulated sugar
- 2 large eggs
- 1 teaspoon vanilla extract
- 1 ripe avocado, mashed
- 1/2 cup milk

Instructions:

1. Preheat the oven to 350°F (175°C). Grease and flour an 8-inch round cake pan.
2. In a bowl, whisk together flour, baking powder, baking soda, and salt.
3. In another bowl, beat butter and sugar until light and fluffy. Add eggs, one at a time, and vanilla.
4. Gradually add the dry ingredients and mix in the mashed avocado and milk, combining until smooth.
5. Pour the batter into the prepared pan and bake for 30-35 minutes, or until a toothpick inserted comes out clean.
6. Let the cake cool before serving.

Torta de Maca (Maca Root Cake)

Ingredients:

- 2 cups all-purpose flour
- 1 teaspoon baking powder
- 1/2 teaspoon salt
- 1/2 cup unsalted butter, softened
- 1 cup brown sugar
- 2 large eggs
- 1 teaspoon vanilla extract
- 1 tablespoon maca root powder
- 1/2 cup milk

Instructions:

1. Preheat the oven to 350°F (175°C). Grease and flour an 8-inch round cake pan.
2. In a bowl, whisk together flour, baking powder, salt, and maca root powder.
3. In another bowl, beat butter and brown sugar until light and fluffy. Add eggs, one at a time, and vanilla.
4. Gradually add the dry ingredients and milk, mixing until smooth.
5. Pour the batter into the prepared pan and bake for 30-35 minutes, or until a toothpick inserted comes out clean.
6. Let the cake cool before serving.

Torta de Quinua (Quinoa Cake)

Ingredients:

- 1 1/2 cups cooked quinoa
- 1 1/2 cups all-purpose flour
- 1 teaspoon baking powder
- 1/2 teaspoon salt
- 1/2 cup unsalted butter, softened
- 1 cup granulated sugar
- 2 large eggs
- 1 teaspoon vanilla extract
- 1/2 cup milk

Instructions:

1. Preheat the oven to 350°F (175°C). Grease and flour an 8-inch round cake pan.
2. In a bowl, whisk together flour, baking powder, and salt.
3. In another bowl, beat butter and sugar until light and fluffy. Add eggs, one at a time, and vanilla.
4. Gradually add the dry ingredients and mix in the cooked quinoa and milk, combining until smooth.
5. Pour the batter into the prepared pan and bake for 30-35 minutes, or until a toothpick inserted comes out clean.
6. Let the cake cool before serving.

Torta de Choclo (Corn Cake)

Ingredients:

- 1 1/2 cups cornmeal
- 1 1/2 teaspoons baking powder
- 1/2 teaspoon salt
- 1/2 cup unsalted butter, softened
- 1 cup sugar
- 3 large eggs
- 1 cup milk
- 1 cup fresh corn kernels (or canned, drained)

Instructions:

1. Preheat the oven to 350°F (175°C). Grease and flour an 8-inch round cake pan.
2. In a bowl, whisk together cornmeal, baking powder, and salt.
3. In another bowl, beat butter and sugar until light and fluffy. Add eggs, one at a time, and mix well.
4. Gradually add the dry ingredients, then add milk, mixing until smooth.
5. Gently fold in the corn kernels.
6. Pour the batter into the prepared pan and bake for 30-35 minutes, or until a toothpick inserted comes out clean.
7. Let the cake cool before serving.

Torta de Higo (Fig Cake)

Ingredients:

- 2 cups all-purpose flour
- 1 1/2 teaspoons baking powder
- 1/2 teaspoon salt
- 1/2 cup unsalted butter, softened
- 1 cup brown sugar
- 2 large eggs
- 1 teaspoon vanilla extract
- 1 1/2 cups chopped dried figs
- 1/2 cup milk

Instructions:

1. Preheat the oven to 350°F (175°C). Grease and flour an 8-inch round cake pan.
2. In a bowl, whisk together flour, baking powder, and salt.
3. In another bowl, beat butter and brown sugar until light and fluffy. Add eggs, one at a time, and vanilla.
4. Gradually add the dry ingredients, then add the chopped figs and milk, mixing until smooth.
5. Pour the batter into the prepared pan and bake for 30-35 minutes, or until a toothpick inserted comes out clean.
6. Let the cake cool before serving.

Torta de Algarrobo (Carob Cake)

Ingredients:

- 2 cups all-purpose flour
- 1 1/2 teaspoons baking powder
- 1/2 teaspoon salt
- 1/2 cup unsalted butter, softened
- 1 cup sugar
- 2 large eggs
- 1 teaspoon vanilla extract
- 1/2 cup carob powder
- 1/2 cup milk

Instructions:

1. Preheat the oven to 350°F (175°C). Grease and flour an 8-inch round cake pan.
2. In a bowl, whisk together flour, baking powder, salt, and carob powder.
3. In another bowl, beat butter and sugar until light and fluffy. Add eggs, one at a time, and vanilla.
4. Gradually add the dry ingredients, then add the milk, mixing until smooth.
5. Pour the batter into the prepared pan and bake for 30-35 minutes, or until a toothpick inserted comes out clean.
6. Let the cake cool before serving.

Torta de Galleta (Cookie Cake)

Ingredients:

- 2 cups all-purpose flour
- 1/2 teaspoon baking soda
- 1/2 teaspoon salt
- 1 cup unsalted butter, softened
- 1 cup brown sugar
- 1 large egg
- 1 teaspoon vanilla extract
- 1 1/2 cups chocolate chips
- 1/2 cup crushed cookies (e.g., Oreos or graham crackers)

Instructions:

1. Preheat the oven to 350°F (175°C). Grease and flour an 8-inch round cake pan.
2. In a bowl, whisk together flour, baking soda, and salt.
3. In another bowl, beat butter and brown sugar until light and fluffy. Add the egg and vanilla, mixing well.
4. Gradually add the dry ingredients, then fold in chocolate chips and crushed cookies.
5. Pour the batter into the prepared pan and bake for 25-30 minutes, or until golden brown and a toothpick comes out clean.
6. Let the cake cool before serving.

Torta de Acelga y Queso (Chard and Cheese Cake)

Ingredients:

- 2 cups all-purpose flour
- 1 teaspoon baking powder
- 1/2 teaspoon salt
- 1/2 cup unsalted butter, softened
- 1 cup granulated sugar
- 2 large eggs
- 1 teaspoon vanilla extract
- 1 1/2 cups cooked chard, finely chopped
- 1/2 cup ricotta cheese
- 1/2 cup grated parmesan cheese
- 1/4 cup milk

Instructions:

1. Preheat the oven to 350°F (175°C). Grease and flour an 8-inch round cake pan.
2. In a bowl, whisk together flour, baking powder, and salt.
3. In another bowl, beat butter and sugar until light and fluffy. Add eggs, one at a time, and vanilla.
4. Gradually add the dry ingredients, then fold in the chopped chard, ricotta, parmesan, and milk. Mix until smooth.
5. Pour the batter into the prepared pan and bake for 30-35 minutes, or until a toothpick inserted comes out clean.
6. Let the cake cool before serving.

Torta de Chocoteja (Chocolate-covered Fruit Cake)

Ingredients:

- 2 cups all-purpose flour
- 1 1/2 teaspoons baking powder
- 1/2 teaspoon salt
- 1/2 cup unsalted butter, softened
- 1 cup brown sugar
- 2 large eggs
- 1 teaspoon vanilla extract
- 1 cup dried fruits (raisins, apricots, etc.), chopped
- 1/2 cup dark chocolate chips
- 1/2 cup milk

Instructions:

1. Preheat the oven to 350°F (175°C). Grease and flour an 8-inch round cake pan.
2. In a bowl, whisk together flour, baking powder, and salt.
3. In another bowl, beat butter and brown sugar until light and fluffy. Add eggs, one at a time, and vanilla.
4. Gradually add the dry ingredients and milk, mixing until smooth.
5. Fold in the chopped dried fruits and chocolate chips.
6. Pour the batter into the prepared pan and bake for 30-35 minutes, or until a toothpick inserted comes out clean.
7. Let the cake cool before serving.

Torta de Lúcuma (Lucuma Cake)

Ingredients:

- 2 cups all-purpose flour
- 1 1/2 teaspoons baking powder
- 1/2 teaspoon salt
- 1/2 cup unsalted butter, softened
- 1 cup granulated sugar
- 2 large eggs
- 1 teaspoon vanilla extract
- 1/2 cup lúcuma puree (or substitute with similar fruit puree)
- 1/4 cup milk

Instructions:

1. Preheat the oven to 350°F (175°C). Grease and flour an 8-inch round cake pan.
2. In a bowl, whisk together flour, baking powder, and salt.
3. In another bowl, beat butter and sugar until light and fluffy. Add eggs, one at a time, and vanilla.
4. Gradually add the dry ingredients, then mix in the lúcuma puree and milk until smooth.
5. Pour the batter into the prepared pan and bake for 30-35 minutes, or until a toothpick inserted comes out clean.
6. Let the cake cool before serving.

Torta de Granadilla (Granadilla Cake)

Ingredients:

- 2 cups all-purpose flour
- 1 1/2 teaspoons baking powder
- 1/2 teaspoon salt
- 1/2 cup unsalted butter, softened
- 1 cup granulated sugar
- 2 large eggs
- 1 teaspoon vanilla extract
- 1/2 cup granadilla pulp (or passion fruit pulp)
- 1/4 cup milk

Instructions:

1. Preheat the oven to 350°F (175°C). Grease and flour an 8-inch round cake pan.
2. In a bowl, whisk together flour, baking powder, and salt.
3. In another bowl, beat butter and sugar until light and fluffy. Add eggs, one at a time, and vanilla.
4. Gradually add the dry ingredients, then mix in the granadilla pulp and milk.
5. Pour the batter into the prepared pan and bake for 30-35 minutes, or until a toothpick inserted comes out clean.
6. Let the cake cool before serving.

Torta de Uchuva (Goldenberry Cake)

Ingredients:

- 2 cups all-purpose flour
- 1 1/2 teaspoons baking powder
- 1/2 teaspoon salt
- 1/2 cup unsalted butter, softened
- 1 cup sugar
- 2 large eggs
- 1 teaspoon vanilla extract
- 1 cup goldenberries (uchuva), chopped or whole
- 1/4 cup milk

Instructions:

1. Preheat the oven to 350°F (175°C). Grease and flour an 8-inch round cake pan.
2. In a bowl, whisk together flour, baking powder, and salt.
3. In another bowl, beat butter and sugar until light and fluffy. Add eggs, one at a time, and vanilla.
4. Gradually add the dry ingredients, then fold in the goldenberries and milk.
5. Pour the batter into the prepared pan and bake for 30-35 minutes, or until a toothpick inserted comes out clean.
6. Let the cake cool before serving.

Torta de Frutos Rojos (Red Fruits Cake)

Ingredients:

- 2 cups all-purpose flour
- 1 1/2 teaspoons baking powder
- 1/2 teaspoon salt
- 1/2 cup unsalted butter, softened
- 1 cup granulated sugar
- 2 large eggs
- 1 teaspoon vanilla extract
- 1 1/2 cups mixed red fruits (raspberries, strawberries, cherries)
- 1/4 cup milk

Instructions:

1. Preheat the oven to 350°F (175°C). Grease and flour an 8-inch round cake pan.
2. In a bowl, whisk together flour, baking powder, and salt.
3. In another bowl, beat butter and sugar until light and fluffy. Add eggs, one at a time, and vanilla.
4. Gradually add the dry ingredients, then fold in the red fruits and milk.
5. Pour the batter into the prepared pan and bake for 30-35 minutes, or until a toothpick inserted comes out clean.
6. Let the cake cool before serving.

Torta de Lentejas (Lentil Cake)

Ingredients:

- 2 cups cooked lentils, mashed
- 1 1/2 cups all-purpose flour
- 1 teaspoon baking powder
- 1/2 teaspoon salt
- 1/2 cup unsalted butter, softened
- 1 cup brown sugar
- 2 large eggs
- 1 teaspoon vanilla extract
- 1/4 cup milk

Instructions:

1. Preheat the oven to 350°F (175°C). Grease and flour an 8-inch round cake pan.
2. In a bowl, whisk together flour, baking powder, and salt.
3. In another bowl, beat butter and sugar until light and fluffy. Add eggs, one at a time, and vanilla.
4. Gradually add the dry ingredients, then mix in the mashed lentils and milk until smooth.
5. Pour the batter into the prepared pan and bake for 30-35 minutes, or until a toothpick inserted comes out clean.
6. Let the cake cool before serving.

Torta de Pargo (Fish Cake)

Ingredients:

- 2 cups cooked and flaked pargo fish
- 2 cups all-purpose flour
- 1 1/2 teaspoons baking powder
- 1/2 teaspoon salt
- 1/2 cup unsalted butter, softened
- 1 cup granulated sugar
- 2 large eggs
- 1 teaspoon vanilla extract
- 1/4 cup milk

Instructions:

1. Preheat the oven to 350°F (175°C). Grease and flour an 8-inch round cake pan.
2. In a bowl, whisk together flour, baking powder, and salt.
3. In another bowl, beat butter and sugar until light and fluffy. Add eggs, one at a time, and vanilla.
4. Gradually add the dry ingredients, then fold in the flaked fish and milk.
5. Pour the batter into the prepared pan and bake for 30-35 minutes, or until a toothpick inserted comes out clean.
6. Let the cake cool before serving.

Torta de Ají Amarillo (Yellow Chili Cake)

Ingredients:

- 2 cups all-purpose flour
- 1 1/2 teaspoons baking powder
- 1/2 teaspoon salt
- 1/2 cup unsalted butter, softened
- 1 cup granulated sugar
- 2 large eggs
- 1 teaspoon vanilla extract
- 2 tablespoons yellow chili paste (ají amarillo)
- 1/4 cup milk

Instructions:

1. Preheat the oven to 350°F (175°C). Grease and flour an 8-inch round cake pan.
2. In a bowl, whisk together flour, baking powder, and salt.
3. In another bowl, beat butter and sugar until light and fluffy. Add eggs, one at a time, and vanilla.
4. Gradually add the dry ingredients, then mix in the ají amarillo paste and milk.
5. Pour the batter into the prepared pan and bake for 30-35 minutes, or until a toothpick inserted comes out clean.
6. Let the cake cool before serving.

Torta de Pargo y Camarones (Fish and Shrimp Cake)

Ingredients:

- 1 lb pargo fish fillets, cooked and flaked
- 1/2 lb shrimp, peeled, deveined, and chopped
- 1 cup all-purpose flour
- 1 1/2 teaspoons baking powder
- 1/2 teaspoon salt
- 1/2 cup unsalted butter, softened
- 1 cup granulated sugar
- 2 large eggs
- 1 teaspoon vanilla extract
- 1/4 cup milk
- 1 tablespoon lemon juice
- 1/2 cup breadcrumbs

Instructions:

1. Preheat the oven to 350°F (175°C). Grease and flour an 8-inch round cake pan.
2. In a bowl, whisk together flour, baking powder, and salt.
3. In another bowl, beat butter and sugar until light and fluffy. Add eggs, one at a time, and vanilla.
4. Gradually add the dry ingredients, then fold in the flaked fish, shrimp, lemon juice, and milk.
5. Stir in breadcrumbs to help the batter bind.
6. Pour the batter into the prepared pan and bake for 35-40 minutes, or until a toothpick inserted comes out clean.
7. Let the cake cool before serving.

Torta de Tamal (Tamal Cake)

Ingredients:

- 2 cups masa harina
- 1 1/2 teaspoons baking powder
- 1/2 teaspoon salt
- 1/2 cup unsalted butter, softened
- 1 cup granulated sugar
- 2 large eggs
- 1 teaspoon vanilla extract
- 1/2 cup chicken or vegetable broth
- 1/2 cup grated cheese (optional)
- 1/2 cup cooked corn kernels (optional)

Instructions:

1. Preheat the oven to 350°F (175°C). Grease and flour an 8-inch round cake pan.
2. In a bowl, whisk together masa harina, baking powder, and salt.
3. In another bowl, beat butter and sugar until light and fluffy. Add eggs, one at a time, and vanilla.
4. Gradually add the dry ingredients and chicken broth, mixing until smooth.
5. Fold in the cheese and corn kernels if using.
6. Pour the batter into the prepared pan and bake for 30-35 minutes, or until a toothpick inserted comes out clean.
7. Let the cake cool before serving.

Torta de Durazno y Maracuyá (Peach and Passion Fruit Cake)

Ingredients:

- 2 cups all-purpose flour
- 1 1/2 teaspoons baking powder
- 1/2 teaspoon salt
- 1/2 cup unsalted butter, softened
- 1 cup granulated sugar
- 2 large eggs
- 1 teaspoon vanilla extract
- 1 cup peach puree
- 1/2 cup passion fruit pulp
- 1/4 cup milk

Instructions:

1. Preheat the oven to 350°F (175°C). Grease and flour an 8-inch round cake pan.
2. In a bowl, whisk together flour, baking powder, and salt.
3. In another bowl, beat butter and sugar until light and fluffy. Add eggs, one at a time, and vanilla.
4. Gradually add the dry ingredients, then fold in the peach puree, passion fruit pulp, and milk.
5. Pour the batter into the prepared pan and bake for 30-35 minutes, or until a toothpick inserted comes out clean.
6. Let the cake cool before serving.

Torta de Choclo y Queso (Corn and Cheese Cake)

Ingredients:

- 2 cups fresh corn kernels
- 1 1/2 cups all-purpose flour
- 1 teaspoon baking powder
- 1/2 teaspoon salt
- 1/2 cup unsalted butter, softened
- 1 cup granulated sugar
- 2 large eggs
- 1 teaspoon vanilla extract
- 1 cup grated cheese (queso fresco or similar)
- 1/4 cup milk

Instructions:

1. Preheat the oven to 350°F (175°C). Grease and flour an 8-inch round cake pan.
2. In a blender or food processor, blend the fresh corn kernels until smooth.
3. In a bowl, whisk together flour, baking powder, and salt.
4. In another bowl, beat butter and sugar until light and fluffy. Add eggs, one at a time, and vanilla.
5. Gradually add the dry ingredients, then fold in the blended corn, grated cheese, and milk.
6. Pour the batter into the prepared pan and bake for 30-35 minutes, or until a toothpick inserted comes out clean.
7. Let the cake cool before serving.

Torta de Frutos Secos (Dried Fruit Cake)

Ingredients:

- 2 cups all-purpose flour
- 1 1/2 teaspoons baking powder
- 1/2 teaspoon salt
- 1/2 cup unsalted butter, softened
- 1 cup brown sugar
- 2 large eggs
- 1 teaspoon vanilla extract
- 1/2 cup mixed dried fruits (raisins, apricots, figs, dates)
- 1/4 cup nuts (walnuts, almonds, or pecans)
- 1/4 cup milk

Instructions:

1. Preheat the oven to 350°F (175°C). Grease and flour an 8-inch round cake pan.
2. In a bowl, whisk together flour, baking powder, and salt.
3. In another bowl, beat butter and brown sugar until light and fluffy. Add eggs, one at a time, and vanilla.
4. Gradually add the dry ingredients, then fold in the dried fruits, nuts, and milk.
5. Pour the batter into the prepared pan and bake for 30-35 minutes, or until a toothpick inserted comes out clean.
6. Let the cake cool before serving.

Torta de Turrón (Nougat Cake)

Ingredients:

- 2 cups all-purpose flour
- 1 1/2 teaspoons baking powder
- 1/2 teaspoon salt
- 1/2 cup unsalted butter, softened
- 1 cup granulated sugar
- 2 large eggs
- 1 teaspoon vanilla extract
- 1/2 cup nougat (chopped into small pieces)
- 1/4 cup milk

Instructions:

1. Preheat the oven to 350°F (175°C). Grease and flour an 8-inch round cake pan.
2. In a bowl, whisk together flour, baking powder, and salt.
3. In another bowl, beat butter and sugar until light and fluffy. Add eggs, one at a time, and vanilla.
4. Gradually add the dry ingredients, then fold in the nougat pieces and milk.
5. Pour the batter into the prepared pan and bake for 30-35 minutes, or until a toothpick inserted comes out clean.
6. Let the cake cool before serving.

Torta de Café y Canela (Coffee and Cinnamon Cake)

Ingredients:

- 2 cups all-purpose flour
- 1 1/2 teaspoons baking powder
- 1/2 teaspoon salt
- 1/2 teaspoon ground cinnamon
- 1/2 cup unsalted butter, softened
- 1 cup granulated sugar
- 2 large eggs
- 1 teaspoon vanilla extract
- 1/2 cup strong brewed coffee, cooled
- 1/4 cup milk

Instructions:

1. Preheat the oven to 350°F (175°C). Grease and flour an 8-inch round cake pan.
2. In a bowl, whisk together flour, baking powder, salt, and cinnamon.
3. In another bowl, beat butter and sugar until light and fluffy. Add eggs, one at a time, and vanilla.
4. Gradually add the dry ingredients, then mix in the coffee and milk until smooth.
5. Pour the batter into the prepared pan and bake for 30-35 minutes, or until a toothpick inserted comes out clean.
6. Let the cake cool before serving.